INCREDIBLE ANIMAL LIFE CYCLES
LIFE CYCLE OF A
JELLYFISH

by Karen Latchana Kenney

pogo

Ideas for Parents and Teachers

Pogo Books let children practice reading informational text while introducing them to nonfiction features such as headings, labels, sidebars, maps, and diagrams, as well as a table of contents, glossary, and index.

Carefully leveled text with a strong photo match offers early fluent readers the support they need to succeed.

Before Reading

- "Walk" through the book and point out the various nonfiction features. Ask the student what purpose each feature serves.

- Look at the glossary together. Read and discuss the words.

Read the Book

- Have the child read the book independently.

- Invite him or her to list questions that arise from reading.

After Reading

- Discuss the child's questions. Talk about how he or she might find answers to those questions.

- Prompt the child to think more. Ask: What did you know about the life cycle of a jellyfish before you read this book? What more would you like to learn after reading it?

Pogo Books are published by Jump!
5357 Penn Avenue South
Minneapolis, MN 55419
www.jumplibrary.com

Library of Congress Cataloging-in-Publication Data

Names: Kenney, Karen Latchana, author.
Title: Life cycle of a jellyfish / by Karen Latchana Kenney.
Description: Minneapolis, MN : Jump!, Inc., [2018]
Series: Incredible animal life cycles
"Pogo Books are published by Jump!"
Audience: Ages 7–10. | Includes index.
Identifiers: LCCN 2017060206 (print)
LCCN 2017059762 (ebook)
ISBN 9781624968143 (ebook)
ISBN 9781624968129 (hardcover : alk. paper)
ISBN 9781624968136 (pbk.)
Subjects: LCSH: Jellyfishes—Life cycles—Juvenile literature.
Classification: LCC QL375.6 (print)
LCC QL375.6 .K46 2018 (ebook) | DDC 593.5/3156—dc23
LC record available at https://lccn.loc.gov/2017060206

Editor: Jenna Trnka
Book Designer: Molly Ballanger

Photo Credits: Rubén Duro/BioMEDIA ASSOCIATES LLC/Science Source, cover (left); Studio 37/Shutterstock, cover (right); Paul Marcellini/Nature Picture Library, 1; IrinaK/Shutterstock, 3; archana bhartia/Shutterstock, 4; Z.H.CHEN/Shutterstock, 5; blickwinkel/Alamy, 6-7; SuperStock, 8-9, 12-13; David Wrobel/Getty, 10-11; Takao Shioguchi/Getty, 14-15; cbimages/Alamy, 16 (left); elnaveante/Shutterstock, 16 (right); Culture RM Exclusive/Alexander Semenov/Getty, 17; George Karbus Photography/Cultura Limited/SuperStock, 18-19; Ethan Daniels/Shutterstock, 20-21; Jiri Vaclavek/Shutterstock, 23.

Printed in the United States of America at Corporate Graphics in North Mankato, Minnesota.

TABLE OF CONTENTS

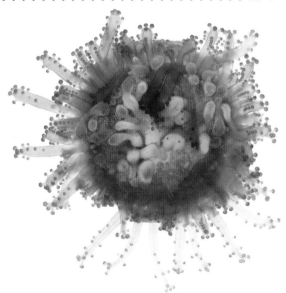

CHAPTER 1

A SEA OF JELLYFISH

In the sea, jellyfish gather in a swarm. They are ready to **spawn**.

The males release **sperm**. It finds a female's eggs in the water. Soon the eggs will grow and change. This is just the beginning of the incredible life cycle of jellyfish.

Each egg looks like a tiny, hairy ball. It is the jellyfish's **planula**, or **larva**. The planulae are too small to see. They float down toward the ocean floor. Why? To find a rock or other surface.

The planulae plant themselves there. They grow into **polyps**.

DID YOU KNOW?

Many polyps grow near each other. They form a **colony**.

polyp colony

tentacles

polyp

Each polyp grows a disc-shaped foot. The foot sticks to the surface. Its body grows upward in a tube shape. Its **tentacles** wave in the water. But it is tiny. How tiny? As small as a pencil tip.

CHAPTER 2

....

BREAKING FREE

The polyp eats and eats. What? **Plankton**. It needs food to grow.

It **absorbs** its tentacles into its body. Then a stack of flat discs grows. It stretches up into the water.

Finally, the top disc twists. It breaks free. It is now an **ephyra**. It pumps its armlike parts up and down. It moves its tiny body through the water.

The ephyra drifts far from where it was born. This is how jellyfish spread to different parts of the ocean.

DID YOU KNOW?

Jellyfish are **invertebrates**. They do not have spines or any bones. They don't have brains either!

ephyra

Soon the ephyrae begin to look like adults. They are **juveniles**. Their bodies become more bell-shaped. Their thin tentacles grow longer. Their arms grow, too.

TAKE A LOOK!

Each jellyfish goes through life cycle **stages**:

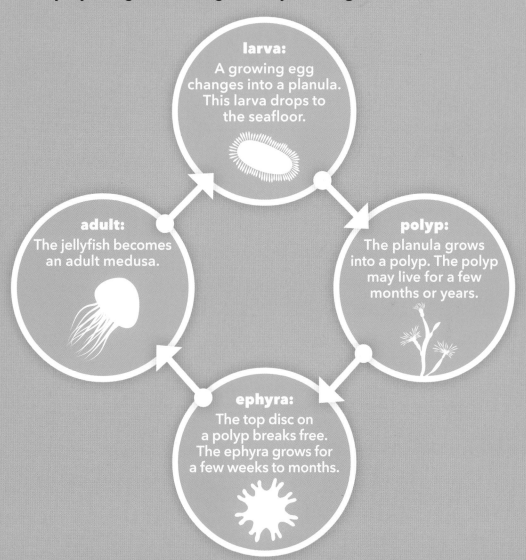

larva:
A growing egg changes into a planula. This larva drops to the seafloor.

polyp:
The planula grows into a polyp. The polyp may live for a few months or years.

ephyra:
The top disc on a polyp breaks free. The ephyra grows for a few weeks to months.

adult:
The jellyfish becomes an adult medusa.

CHAPTER 3

A STINGING MEDUSA

Now the jellyfish is an adult medusa. Some don't grow big at all. A thimble sea jellyfish is smaller than a penny.

Others are very large. The lion's mane jellyfish can be 8 feet (2.4 meters) across. Their tentacles stretch close to the length of an airplane!

Tentacles are a medusa's best weapon. They can shoot out stinging threads. The threads are filled with toxic **venom**. It stings **prey**. The prey stops moving. Then the jellyfish pulls it into its mouth with its arms.

TAKE A LOOK!

Here are the parts of an adult jellyfish's body. The bell moves up and down to move itself forward. The mouth is in the bell, too. Long tentacles sting prey. Arms pull prey to the mouth.

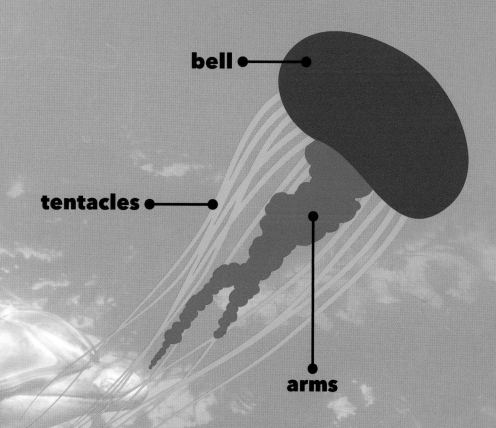

bell

tentacles

arms

When they are ready, many medusae gather. The males release sperm. The females' eggs start growing. And soon new planulae fall to the seafloor. They begin growing into new jellyfish. One day they'll be swimming medusae, too.

DID YOU KNOW?

Many jellyfish are clear, making them hard to see in the water. But others have very bright colors. Some even glow in the dark!

ACTIVITIES & TOOLS

JELLYFISH LOOK-ALIKE

Some animals eat jellyfish. But plastic bags pollute the ocean. Animals think they are jellyfish and eat them instead. See how a plastic bag can look like a jellyfish with this activity.

What You Need:

- clear plastic grocery bag
- clear refillable water bottle
- rubber band
- food coloring
- scissors

1. Lay the bag flat. Cut off the handles and bottom.

2. Cut along both sides to split it into two sheets. Discard one sheet.

3. Pick up the other sheet. Pull up a bunch in the middle to make a head. Wrap the rubber band around it.

4. Cut tentacles out of the hanging part of the bag. Cut as many as you want. You can trim them for different lengths, too.

5. Pour some water into the head part. Be sure to leave a little bit of air so it floats.

6. Fill up your water bottle and add a couple drops of food coloring.

7. Put your jellyfish in the bottle. Screw on the cap tight.

8. Turn the bottle upside down to watch the jellyfish swim! Notice how its tentacles move.

GLOSSARY

absorbs: Gradually takes something in.

colony: A large group of creatures that lives together.

ephyra: A baby jellyfish that breaks off a polyp.

invertebrates: Creatures that do not have spines.

juveniles: Young jellyfish that are close to being adults.

larva: A jellyfish in a stage between an egg and polyp.

plankton: Small animals and plants that float in the ocean.

planula: A growing jellyfish egg that looks like a hairy ball.

polyps: Stages when the jellyfish have tube-shaped bodies that stick to the seafloor.

prey: An animal that is hunted by another animal for food.

spawn: To release eggs.

sperm: A male animal's cells that make a female's eggs start growing into babies.

stages: Steps or periods of development.

tentacles: Long, moving limbs of a jellyfish.

venom: A poison that harms prey.

INDEX

TO LEARN MORE

Learning more is as easy as 1, 2, 3.

1) Go to www.factsurfer.com

2) Enter "lifecycleofajellyfish" into the search box.

3) Click the "Surf" button to see a list of websites.

With factsurfer, finding more information is just a click away.